ROMOLA & NIJINSKY

Deux Mariages

Lynne Alvarez

BROADWAY PLAY PUBLISHING INC
New York
www.broadwayplaypub.com
info@broadwayplaypub.com

ROMOLA & NIJINSKY

Cover art by Brian T Whitehill

First printing:September 2004
This printing, revised: July 2018
I S B N: 978-0-88145-235-8

Book design: Marie Donovan
Page make-up: Adobe Indesign
Typeface: Palatino

ROMOLA & NIJINSKY was first produced on 20 April 2003 by Primary Stages (Casey Childs, Executive Producer; Andrew Leynse, Artistic Director). The cast and creative contributors were:

ROMOLA .... Kelly Hutchinson
NIJINSKY .... David Barlow
BARON .... Allen Fitzpatrick
EMILIA & ANNA .... Janet Zarish
DIAGHELIFF / VASSILY .... Daniel Oreskes
THE MAN WITH THE PIPE .... John Mcadams
DANCERS .... Michelle Lookadoo, Laura Martin, & Matt Rivera

Director .... David Levine
Choreography .... Robert La Fosse
Set design .... Michael Byrnes
Costume design .... Claudia Stephens
Lighting design .... Lao-Chi Chu
Sound design .... Jane Shaw
Original composition .... Brendan Connelly
Prop design .... Laurie Marvald
Production stage manager .... Erika Timperman
Assistant stage manager .... Diane M Ballering
Production manager .... Lester P Grant
Production consultant .... Fran Kirmser
Assistant directors .... Kathryn Moroney & Loe Mackler
Casting .... Stephanie Klapper
Press representative .... Jeffrey Richards Associates

Special funding for the production was provided by The Peter Jay Sharp Foundation and The Russell Fellowship for Playwrights.

CHARACTERS & SETTING

ROMOLA DE PULSKY, *twenty, dancer in the Corps de Ballet of the Ballets Russes*

VASLAV NIJINSKY, *twenty-one, soloist and star of the Ballet Russes*

BARON DIMITRI DE GUNSBOURG, *forty-five, Russian aristocrat, major backer and Acting-Director of the Ballets Russes on tour*

EMILIA MARKUS, *forty-five, great Hungarian classical actress and* ROMOLA'*s mother*

SERGEI DIAGHELIFF, *forty-five, creator and Director of the Ballets Russes, formerly* NIJINSKY'*s lover and mentor.*

ANNA, *forty,* ROMOLA'*s companion/attendant*

VASSILY, *sixty,* DIAGHELIFF'*s valet passed on to* NIJINSKY

THE MAN WITH THE PIPE (RUPERT), *anywhere from thirty to sixty. English passenger, polymorphos, perverse*

Three DANCERS, *two women and one man*

The DANCERS *play all minor roles including, the ship's captain, maids, waiters, prostitutes, the priest and couples promenading on deck etc. regardless of gender. The* DANCERS *should preferably be ballet dancers and do some of their movements on point. There are several full dance numbers as indicated in the script and at times the dancers do have minimal lines to say. However—despite the particular character they may portray in any given moment—they should first and foremostvbe seen as dancers portraying a role, i.e. they should walk like dancers, should feel free to do dance steps as they move about and their costumes might be fitted rather obviously over their basic dance outfits and shoes. Since these dancers are mischievous and sometimes worse—their basic costume should reflect this. Please use the dancers to augment, mirror, introduce or bridge action on stage although with the caveat that they do not either crowd or intrude upon the ongoing action of the play or the intimacy of any scenes. Dancing should be given as much separate emphasis as the dialogue. The written play, in many regards but not all, is much like the libretto of an opera where the dance often plays the part of the music.*

We never *see* NIJINSKY *dance.*

Variously—a ballroom in Saint Moritz, Switzerland on January 19, 1919; aboard the S S Avon *during the month of August 1913; a church in Buenos Aires on September 10, 1913. Sets are optional.*

ACT ONE

Prologue

(January 19, 1919. A private home. Saint Moritz, Switzerland. A night sky. Instead of stars we gradually realize there are a variety of eyes overhead: some blinking, some staring, some human and others of animals. NIJINSKY *is in a circle of light. He is wearing practical clothes. Far upstage right in another spot of light is a dancer dressed as* NIJINSKY *doing Petrouschka. He dances. At some point during* NIJINSKY*'s speech, he turns and turns and turns and turns and turns and disappears.)*

(Some characters enter with chairs facing the audience—as if the audience is the performance. ROMOLA *enters beautifully, elegantly dressed with her mother,* EMILIA. DIAGHELIFF *enters in tails. They sit. We hear the opening of* Petrouschka.*)*

*(*ROMOLA *bends toward* EMILIA *and whispers. Her voice, however, is projected over the music and dancing.)*

ROMOLA: This is the greatest role, *ma mere*, exquisite. Petrouschka dies, of course.
For love, what else is there? Watch him, how he suffers, how he extends with a trembling arm his agony and sadness to the only people who understand him—the gray common crowd of Russia. Is it not extraordinary how he seems to be made of wood and yet executes the most difficult steps? Look at those pirouettes and *toures en l'air*. Perfect, perfect, but always in character. And

you will see the suffering of this doll, Petrouschka. In his last breath, even, Petrouschka's heart is filled with love for the ballerina. He sends her his last tragic kiss. See how he presses the palm of his hand to his pale lips and trembling, jerking...see...see how he does it! He extends his arm toward the vastness of space. Oh, yes. *(She stands.) Bravo, bravissimo.*

(Everyone stands and claps as the music does not stop, but repeats.)

ROMOLA: But what's wrong?

EMILIA: He is still dancing!

DIAGHELIFF: Stop, Vatza!

ROMOLA: Oh, Vaslav, stop!

(End of Prologue)

Scene One

(It is August 1913.We are on the S S Avon *heading to South America. Piquant music. The scene begins with a 2:32 minute dance which establishes being aboard ship. First there is a "pas de trois" with the Captain and two passengers who arrive. Tickets are requested and checked, boxes carried etc. other passengers arrive cross, meet and acknowledge each other or not. The dancers wave to people on shore. Point out things of interest, jostling each other for a better view and competing for the captain's attention. The dancers are always dancing—very mannered, very turn of the century ballet—while the other passengers are walking naturally, promenading on deck in character. The* BARON, *organizing other people, the man with the pipe flirting with anything that moves—but especially the* BARON *and* ANNA *when the* BARON *isn't looking.* ROMOLA *and* ANNA *enter.)*

ROMOLA: Of course he's extreme Anna. He's a genius and he's Russian!

(One of the dancers sees something in the sky and drops to her knees and crosses herself. She points it out to the other dancer who crosses herself many times.)

ANNA: Barbarians! They're all mad if you ask me. Impossibly superstitious. My God if a crow flies overhead—they're all on their knees crossing themselves.

(The Englishman smoking a pipe walks by.)

ANNA: I think I will learn to smoke a pipe.

ROMOLA: I can't believe you like that Englishman. He's so common!

ANNA: Shhhhhhh.

ROMOLA: He doesn't understand Hungarian, Anna. No one understands Hungarian.
Now come over here. Look at the ocean. It's endless.

ANNA: It moves too much

ROMOLA: It's lovely. I hope Buenos Aires will have beaches like they do in Italy—with all those dark men following us whispering obscenities.

ANNA: I'm going to follow my Englishman.

ROMOLA: What? You?

ANNA: Yes. Romola. I have decided to take advantage of this voyage. I shall follow my heart for once. I may be an old maid—but I needn't have an unscathed hymen as well!

*(*NIJINSKY *enters. He is followed by* VASSILY *holding a towel and watering can.* NIJINSKY *is stopped by admirers.* VASSILY *takes the moment to wipe away* NIJINSKY*'s perspiration.)*

ROMOLA: Anna!
You can't go.

ANNA: Yes I can.

ROMOLA: No. *Le Petit.*

ANNA: Please!

ROMOLA: You can't leave me now. I need you.
Thank you Divine Child for allowing me to live in this century and to have seen Nijinsky dance!
How do I look?

ANNA: Awful.

ROMOLA: Is he looking at me? (*She laughs loudly, posing.*)

ANNA: No.

ROMOLA: Wait!

(ROMOLA *takes out a cigarette.* ANNA *reluctantly lights it.*)

ANNA: Those Turkish things. Oh that should make a wonderful impression. Now we'll both smell like camel dung. Blow the smoke the other way.

ROMOLA: Is he watching yet?

ANNA: No.

ROMOLA: What's he doing?

ANNA: He's stopped practicing and Vassily is wiping his armpits.

ROMOLA: I must be mad—I want to kiss him there. Yes. And in that cleft under his lower lip where perhaps no one has ever kissed him before.

(ROMOLA *blows out a plume of smoke and* VASSILY *approaches angrily.*)

VASSILY: Away! Away! Go! Very bad!

ROMOLA: What did he say? He speaks French like a barking dog.

ANNA: He wants us to leave.

ROMOLA: Yes Vassily. All right.

*(*ROMOLA *makes a great show of putting out her cigarette.* VASSILY *turns to leave and she says very loudly.)*

ROMOLA: Vassily's such a little old lady with his little towel and watering can. He probably accompanies Vaslav to the loo and wipes his bottom.

ANNA: Hush!

ROMOLA: They don't understand Hungarian.

ANNA: Well don't say their names. They understand that!

ROMOLA: (*Walking by* NIJINSKY *who still doesn't glace her way.)* How rude.
He hasn't given me a glance. I can't stand it. You'd think he never saw me before. But he was so attentive in Budapest when he mistook me for the *prima ballerina* of the Hungarian Opera. I allowed him to kiss my hand— even though he looked like some poor Japanese student with that Tartar face and ill-fitting clothes. But—oh—he moved like a tiger—so soft and fierce. Now he's impossible! I'll show him I can ignore him too. (*She laughs.)* Of course—first he has to notice me ignoring him! Oh please, Miraculous Jesus of Prague, Divine Child—be with me every minute. Let me move like a feather, like an angel, like a drum. I know the only way to his heart is through the dance!

*(*ROMOLA *drags* ANNA *off.* VASSILY *drapes a towel around* NIJINSKY*'s shoulders as they exit, but one of the* DANCERS *snatches it and smells it and shares it with the other. They exit. We hear the slow rise and fall of the ocean against the ship. A couple walks by. The woman is angry and precedes the man with a pipe who is pleading with her. They exit. The lights darken. The* BARON *enters wearing a white linen suit, humming parts of the firebird. He stops to conduct when he comes to an especially lively passage. He wraps a bright shawl around his waist as he continues on to* NIJINSKY*'s cabin.)*

(End of Scene One)

Scene Two

*(*NIJINSKY *is sitting on the massage table as the masseur gathers up his things. The masseur has an interesting "tic". When the masseur's back is turned,* NIJINSKY *studies his movements and tries to reproduce them. There is a knock on the door.)*

BARON: Vasla, Vaslav, may I come in? It is I, Dimitri.

NIJINSKY: What's the matter?

BARON: I can't bear to be alone.

NIJINSKY: It's only an hour to dinner.

BARON: I know, I know.

(The masseur opens the door and the BARON *enters. The masseur gives a slight bow and a dance step and leaves. The* BARON *notices* NIJINSKY *doing the imitation.)*

BARON: What is it? What's wrong? Vaslav, are you having a fit? Oh, I see you're doing one of your studies. Well you do look just like that man, but why would you want to? You should do me? Oh no, that would be too pathetic. But tell me, how do I look? I tried this sash for a bit of color and dash, as we are going to South America. *Olé*. Oh, I can just imagine what your dear Sergei would say, "Dimitri, you look like an aging whore." Odd, I don't miss him, but I'm always quoting him. How indelicate. Personally, I think this separation from Sergei will do you wonders, not that I don't understand your relationship. I had one myself, very romantic, rose petals on the bed, that sort of thing. But, I knew it was doomed. He would always arrive from Kiev with this very small valise. I'd take one look at that very small valise and think, "He's already planning to leave". I felt deserted as soon as he arrived.

NIJINSKY: Please don't talk about love, Dimitri.

BARON: Yes, of course. Passion is nothing but an inferno. Except for dance, of course.

NIJINSKY: Of course.

BARON: Ah, dance. You are so brilliant!

NIJINSKY: You are so transparent. What is it you want, Dimitri?

BARON: I think it's time you rethought your relationship with Diagheliff. I know how deathly tired you are of all his intrigue. Sergei runs the Ballets Russes like a Caliph's court, full of favorites and concubines.

NIJINSKY: Yes.

BARON: Yes well…I have a thought— You and I should start a small company. We could achieve some interesting results, don't you think? No. No. No. Don't answer me now. Think about it. In the meantime, let's play. I have it in mind to introduce you to someone who is quite rich and quite mad for you.

NIJINSKY: I'm not interested. Thank you, Baron.

BARON: Come. Come. The cure for disenchantment is love. If you're interested in girls, there's a beautiful girl on board I think you should meet. She's taken every opportunity to drape herself in front of you. You must have noticed.

NIJINSKY: The blue-eyed girl?

BARON: Yes, yes. That's her.

NIJINSKY: Is she a dancer?

BARON: In the *corps de ballet*, I believe.

NIJINSKY: But the *corps de ballet* is in second class and this girl has a cabin near mine.

BARON: Oh, she's very rich. Her mother is a great classical actress, the premier actress of Hungary, actually. Some say she is as great as Bernhardt. (*Whispering*) She was the seventh child of a button manufacturer.

NIJINSKY: The blue-eyed girl?

BARON: No, her mother. But she became a great actress and married de Pulsky, an aristocrat, which in turn made her very wealthy, which in turn made Romola, that is the blue-eyed girl, a beneficiary of the money. What I am trying to say is, she has money and you should meet her.

NIJINSKY: Does she dance well?

BARON: I can't say. I've never seen her dance. She's only just joined the company for this tour.

NIJINSKY: I could never be interested in any girl who wasn't a beautiful dancer.

BARON: Oh for heaven's sakes—why limit yourself to *prima ballerinas*? You should meet this girl. She's quite pretty and has eyes like sapphires. Perhaps she is a good dancer. Who knows? I will introduce you.

NIJINSKY: No need.

BARON: But why?

NIJINSKY: We've already met.

BARON: I see.

NIJINSKY: Yes.

BARON: Sooo...you hate her.

NIJINSKY: Oh no.

BARON: But you never greet her and she never greets you.

NIJINSKY: I make a display of not noticing her.

BARON: For God's sakes why? She's from a very good family.

NIJINSKY: I enjoy provoking her to flirt. It's always a pleasure to watch someone do what they do best. I'm perfectly happy Baron, to observe love like a beautiful painting of a landscape. It's enchanting and I don't have to inhabit it!

BARON: Pity.

NIJINSKY: You seem awfully determined that we should meet. And why is that, Dimitri? Do you want her to come between me and Sergei Pavlovitch? Will she give her riches to our new company?

BARON: No, I would never presume…

NIJINSKY: I am the Ballets Russes. I would never desert her.

BARON: What if she deserts you?

NIJINSKY: What do you mean? Why do you say that?

BARON: Sergei doesn't really appreciate your choreography the way he should. I adored *Sacre* and *Jeux*—although I admit not many others did. And he wasn't very fond of *L'Apres Midi.*

NIJINSKY: Why? What have you heard?

BARON: Actually I heard that he refuses to give *Faune* in Paris. He said: "It's not a ballet. I'd sooner dismiss the company before I give it again!" But then—perhaps it's all gossip. You know what a shallow bitch I am.

NIJINSKY: So shallow, but so clever. Well! I leave you to your motives and ask you to take me on deck and show me how to smoke a pipe like a proper Englishman.

BARON: A pipe? What makes you think I know…? Oh… Ohhhh. Yes, oh, so you saw me with that lovely gentleman. He's quite impressive and he knows everything about Hindu ruins. He's been hunting with a minor *maharajah*. He's wild about animals, so sensitive. He told me he would give his soul if, just once, he could watch an elephant drink. He's offered to take me on safari through the jungles of the Amazon—but I can't possibly go. Suppose the relationship is brief? Safari clothes are so costly and it would be a perfect waste of money to have them made if the relationship were brief. I mean, where else could I use them? Certainly not with my wife.

(End of Scene Two)

Scene Three

(ROMOLA *and* ANNA *are sitting on deck chairs.* ROMOLA *is daydreaming with a book in her lap and* ANNA *is carefully putting on lotion. The* MAN WITH THE PIPE *walks by. He greets both ladies but he is eyeing* ANNA.)

MAN WITH THE PIPE: Good day, *mademoiselles*. Lovely morning.

ANNA: A fine day to you, too, *Monsieur.*

(Their eyes linger.)

MAN WITH THE PIPE: This equatorial sun is terribly hot, don't you think?

ANNA: Have we crossed the equator, then?

MAN WITH THE PIPE: No. Tonight. Is this your first time?

ANNA: First time…?

MAN WITH THE PIPE: Crossing.

ANNA: Oh, yes, and yours?

MAN WITH THE PIPE: My third.

ANNA: Oh.

MAN WITH THE PIPE: Yes, they'll give you little silk flags of all the nations that touch the equator.

(The BARON *and* NIJINSKY *are promenading on the deck. They walk by and the* BARON *gives the* MAN WITH THE PIPE *a flirtatious look. The* MAN WITH THE PIPE *turns his back coldly and obviously.)*

MAN WITH THE PIPE: Yes...well, ladies, enjoy your morning. (*He continues to walk.)*

ROMOLA: Was that him?

ANNA: Who?

ROMOLA: Please. I saw that look pass between you. If you ask me, he was altogether too familiar.

ANNA: Yes, I'll go tell him at once. (*She gets up.)*

ROMOLA: I can't believe you're going to follow him?

ANNA: I have no time to lose.

ROMOLA: But what do you know about him?

ANNA: He's shown interest in me. He's English and he smokes a pipe. I'll tell you more about him when I get back. Ta!

ROMOLA: Go! Leave me alone then, you hussy!

*(*ANNA *exits in the direction of the man.* ROMOLA *takes up a book. Two women prostitutes walk by in deep discussion.)*

WOMAN 2: Pickles and vodka?

WOMAN 1: But he has an estate.

WOMAN 2: I suppose you can't resist.

WOMAN 1: I don't know. The village is backward, the peasants are drunk, and the roads are impassable.

(The women sit. ROMOLA *is restless. The* BARON *and* NIJINSKY *enter and* ROMOLA *ostentatiously raises her book to read. The* BARON *is laughing as* NIJINSKY *is imitating the* MAN WITH THE PIPE.*)*

BARON: Yes, yes that is him! I swear it is him down to the annoying way he holds his pipe. He is pretentious, isn't he? I don't know why the English are so determined to be thought eccentric. I mean, did he think it was attractive? All those bizarre stories about mysterious fires and prominent social figures beaten to death with polo mallets? I refuse to take him seriously.

NIJINSKY: He seemed to like you well enough.

BARON: Please! And when he said, "Dimitri, if you ever want to commit suicide, do it in my arms..." Oh, look, there's that lovely girl. Shall we say hello?

(The BARON *doesn't wait for a response and heads over to* ROMOLA *who feigns distraction.* NIJINSKY *goes to the ship's rail. He is followed by the two prostitutes.)*

BARON: What are you reading, my dear?

ROMOLA: Baron, you startled me.

*(*NIJINSKY *smiles and approaches.)*

ROMOLA: Anna Karenina.

(The BARON *takes it and shows it to* NIJINSKY.*)*

BARON: Look, she is reading a Russian novel, Anna Karenina, by Tolstoy.

NIJINSKY: *(Takes it rather brusquely and looks at it and gives it back. To* BARON*)* In French! *(To* ROMOLA*)* You love Tolstoy?

ROMOLA: Monsieur said something about Tolstoy?

*(*NIJINSKY *and* ROMOLA *exchange smiles.)*

BARON: He asked what you thought of the book.

ROMOLA: Actually, I'm very annoyed with Tolstoy—He made Anna Karenina into such a ninny.

NIJINSKY: *(To* BARON*)* She doesn't like Tolstoy. *(To* ROMOLA*)* Tolstoy, my hero!

BARON: I'm sure you misunderstood...

(NIJINSKY *walks away and looks out to sea.)*

BARON: (*To* ROMOLA*)* He speaks so little French.... Now where did he go? Let me introduce you.

ROMOLA: Never mind, Dimitri. He obviously is more interested in the ocean.

BARON: Oh, you know how he is...the artist.

ROMOLA: No, Baron, really don't bother.

BARON: Why? Are you afraid of him? He may be *Le Dieu de la Dance* on-stage, but off stage he's a charming young man.

ROMOLA: I'm not afraid of him.

BARON: Good. Then let me present him to you.

ROMOLA: I don't care to, Baron. Thank you.

BARON: Don't be silly. You admire him.

ROMOLA: Do I?

BARON: Please! He's captivating. We all admire him. He won't harm you. I promise. We are great pals.

ROMOLA: No. I'm just sick of it. I've been presented to him over and over again and he never remembers me.

BARON: Vaslav Fomitch.

(NIJINSKY *approaches smiling.)*

BARON: So! *Monsieur* Nijinsky, *permettez-moi de vous presenter Mademoiselle* De Pulsky. Her mother is the greatest classical actress in Hungary.

(ROMOLA *extends her hand and* NIJINSKY *takes it.)*

BARON: *Mademoisellle* De Pulsky is a very talented dancer in our *corps de ballet.*

NIJINSKY: Yes.

ROMOLA: Yes…Yes…Oh! *Monsieur* Nijinsky, I must thank you.

NIJINSKY: Thank me?

ROMOLA: Oh, yes, for *Printemps*, for *Sacre.*

NIJINSKY: You are welcome.

ROMOLA: You've made dance the highest art. No matter what they say—never lose your nerve! Do you understand me?

(The BARON *begins to translate but* NIJINSKY *stops him.)*

ROMOLA: All great art begins as blasphemy!

NIJINSKY: Very interesting girl. She has many opinions.

BARON: Very astute and so well read…quite comfortable income.

ROMOLA: (*Looking straight at* NIJINSKY*)* So, gentlemen, do I meet with your approval this time?

(They stare at each other.)

BARON: Sorry. These language difficulties, you know…

NIJINSKY: I want to see her arch.

BARON: I can hardly ask her that!

NIJINSKY: Yes!

BARON: No.

NIJINSKY: (*To* ROMOLA*)* Please, *mademoiselle*—your foot.

BARON: He wants to examine your arch.

ROMOLA: I don't think so.

NIJINSKY: Please.

(NIJINSKY *kisses* ROMOLA*'s hand.)*

ROMOLA: All right

*(*ROMOLA *extends her foot for* NIJINSKY *to take off her shoe. He does and examines her foot for flexibility. It is rather painful.)*

BARON: You know, I must tell you. We've decided to have a costume ball this evening to celebrate crossing the equator. I hope you'll come. Perhaps I shall be an *odalisque* and, Romola Carlovna, I have a brilliant idea for you. You are so slim. You almost look like a boy, (*He examines her.)* and if you hide your hair, I will loan you a pair of my green silk pajamas.

ROMOLA: And what will you wear, *Monsieur* Nijinsky?

*(*NIJINSKY *drops* ROMOLA*'s foot. He stands gives a brief smile and bow and exits.)*

BARON: I hate artists! (*Laughs uneasily)* Yes, well, he's a bit rough around the edges. I shall have to mention that to him. Well then—when you write her—regards to your mother. Brrrrr—she's a real tiger, isn't she?

*(*ANNA *returns.)*

BARON: Good day, Anna. (*He exits.)*

ROMOLA: Anna, guess what? *Le Petit* came over and flirted with me and I looked into his eyes. They're slanted, just like my pet Siamese. His eyes aren't green as I thought on-stage. They're a soft, soft brown, like velvet.

(Eyes appear in the sky like stars. As the lights darken, some are cat's eyes, others are human. Some stare, some blink. We see NIJINSKY *asleep in his cabin.)*

(End of Scene Three)

Scene Four

(The giant eyes, blinking and non-blinking become even more pronounced. We can make out NIJINSKY'*s figure lying on the bed and another figure in formal attire sitting at the foot of the bed. The figure reaches over and pours some water from a flask at* NIJINSKY'*s bedside.* NIJINSKY *stirs. He is still dressed in his practice clothes and reaches blindly for the water.)*

DIAGHELIFF: Is this what you're looking for?

(NIJINSKY *is horrified and doesn't move.)*

DIAGHELIFF: One really shouldn't nap in the afternoon. It's such a heavy sleep and one becomes so disoriented, don't you think?

(DIAGHELIFF *hands the glass to* NIJINSKY *who drinks from it.)*

DIAGHELIFF: But my dear, you know you wanted to see me. Here. Drink. Drink.

NIJINSKY: You have a new boy anyway. Go away. (*He gulps down some water and lights some lights.)*

DIAGHELIFF: I'm still here. Of course, you are seeing things. Perhaps, you've lost control of your mind. Ah, *mon cher*, careful, you are beginning to remind me of your crazy brother, Stassik. Poor soul. (*He looks around the cabin.)* Those eyes are making me nervous. You're not becoming paranoid, are you?

(DIAGHELIFF *snaps his fingers and the eyes disappear.)*

NIJINSKY: I know what an eye is. An eye is a theater.

DIAGHELIFF: Shush, Vatza, shush.

NIJINSKY: I am sick at heart, Sergei. I am tired of intrigue and intrigue. I want to be an unnecessary man. I want to be a monk and build a simple house. I want to go to Siberia and preach to the peasants and work the land. I want to be a tree and its roots. I want to live simply, in isolation.

DIAGHELIFF: You must stop reading that old lunatic, Tolstoy. All this "philosophy". You are getting so boring, Vatza. I want you to take some time off, but for God's sake, use it creatively. Remember we must do something astonishing for Paris next year. Tolstoy! You would go back to the Stone Age at a time when we can't afford to be less modern. No! Futurism, cubism—the soul splintered from the universe—these are the last words. I will not let the position of artistic leadership slip away from me.

NIJINSKY: It's too late. You've already become the ultimate lackey a servile follower, you, the visionary, are now terrified of causing the least scandal.

DIAGHELIFF: You only say this because I thought your ballet *Jeux* was a complete failure. Even your *Sacre du Printemps* is not a real ballet... And *L'Apres Midi*—an eleven-minute ballet that needs a hundred hours of rehearsal. My God. All our friends of the Ballets Russes agree with me. It would be a mistake to encourage you further as a choreographer.

NIJINSKY: *Jeux* was not entirely successful. But, *Sacre* was important.

DIAGHELIFF: The public, the paying public booed it.

NIJINSKY: It's new. It was not understood.

DIAGHELIFF: Vatza, Vatza. A painting or a piece of music might be misunderstood at first or unappreciated for a long time, maybe a hundred years, but a ballet? A ballet must be received by the public today or else it is doomed to obscurity. Come, come I have given you three ballets to choreograph and they are simply not the kind of Ballets that can sustain the success of the Ballets Russes. You must understand that I have a great obligation.

NIJINSKY: But not to me.

DIAGHELIFF: Of course to you, darling. In fact I want you to look at some new ballets Fokine is choreographing and give me your opinion.

NIJINSKY: Fokine?

DIAGHELIFF: Yes.That is, if you have time. I must remember to tell that idiot, De Gunsbourg, to keep the little Hungarian flirt away from you. That imbecile. Does he really think he can separate the two of us with a socialite? He's plotting to have his own company again, but I am hardly worried. That man couldn't run a flea circus.

NIJINSKY: I don't think as little of women as you do, Sergei.

DIAGHELIFF: My poor little saint. How you suffer.

NIJINSKY: There is a difference between what I do for others and what I do for myself.

(Two DANCERS *dressed as prostitutes dance out laughing raucously and approach first* NIJINSKY *and then turn to fawn over* DIAGHELIFF, *who treats them with bored indifference.)*

DIAGHELIFF: Really?

NIJINSKY: Those long solitary walks in Paris? I was looking for whores. I wanted beautiful, healthy girls. I fucked whores every day. Once I made love to a woman who had her period. I was covered with it. Then I went to you because I knew it would disgust you. I lied to you. I became you, a fake, a fraud. You dye your hair black so no one will know you are old, but I know you're old. I see that disgusting black cream you leave on the pillowcases and the lock of hair you dye white just to be noticed—it has turned yellow. Yellow. You have two false front teeth and when you take them out, you look like a wicked old woman. And that monocle you wear is only for effect. Your eyes are perfect. Deceit is your art. Deceit and sex.

DIAGHELIFF: You didn't seem to mind the sex, as I recall. Actually, as I was telling Prince Lvov when he passed you on to me, I was quite gratified by all the nice tricks he taught you. He was a very athletic young man, wasn't he?

NIJINSKY: He understood love. He wrote love poems. He was beautiful. He thought you would be useful to me.

DIAGHELIFF: Yes. His was a great love. He passed you around like a used penny. And I—who corrupted you, who used you—as you claim—made you a god. *Le dieu de la danse.* Vatza, you are a great artist, a gentle soul. Who else can appreciate you as I do?

NIJINSKY: You appreciate me like a painting in a museum. Museums are graveyards! They are tidy. They are dead. Beauty for me isn't tidy. It's not pretty. Beauty is feeling in a face. Beauty is a hunchback. I like ugly people. I am an ugly man with feeling. I dance hunchbacks and straight-backs. I am the artist who loves all shapes and all kinds of beauty.

DIAGHELIFF: Then you must love me, too.

NIJINSKY: I have found a girl. She has chestnut hair, her nose is long and straight. It has character. Her eyes are alive. I want to fuck her.

DIAGHELIFF: What are you doing, Vatza? I am worried to death about you.

NIJINSKY: Of course. You, who thought I was boring and stupid. Who was ashamed I would speak and humiliate you in front of your brilliant friends. I hated you. But I loved the Ballets Russes. I gave my whole heart to the Ballets Russes. I worked like an ox. I lived like a martyr. I killed myself for the dance, but I am tired. Tired. So tired of you showing that Nijinsky is your pupil in everything. I was tired of looking for love when there was nothing. You love fame, you love boys, you love a beautiful body, and you love *objets d'art*. You are wicked. You are crazy. I carry you with me like a stone, like a cross I can't put down. Leave me alone so I can breathe. I am going to the New World. I will have a new life and will do what God asks me.

(DIAGHELIFF *exits.* VASSILY *enters.)*

VASSILY: Vatza,Vatza. (*He fills a glass with water.)* Here drink. There is nothing to be afraid of. Nothing.

NIJINSKY: (*Sobbing)* You are not wicked. I will weep for you if you are ever hurt. I do not like you, but you are a human being and I love all human beings. I have no right to judge. The judge is God and he will whisper in my ear what to do, what to do…

VASSILY: Shall I make more light in the room?

NIJINSKY: What? No.

VASSILY: Here, let me wipe your face. You're sweating. You had a dream? You had a nightmare? …There… there…all will be well, you'll see. Do you want to go to the costume ball? Yes? Shall I lay out your choices. You should never sleep in the afternoon. It is a heavy, unhealthy sleep. I will open a porthole. Here…drink Vatza. Water will cleanse you.

(End of Scene Four)

Scene Five

(The party. We hear music. A crowd gathers. A tango is begun. Suddenly, we see a figure spotlighted center stage. The figure is dressed in classic tango clothes. However, only the right half is dressed as a man, the left half is dressed as a woman; we believe it is only a man dancing. There is a dramatic turn and then the female side is turned toward the audience. The man/woman does a solo tango in which he first seduce some of the dancers as a man and then the other as a woman. Then the three pair off with the other passengers. They all tango. This dance should last about two minutes.)

(As the tango is ending, NIJINSKY *enters. He is not in costume but in evening clothes looking very elegant. The lights come up and we see a circle of grotesquely costumed party goers.* DIAGHELIFF *with the large papier-maché head is there also. Someone is dressed as a bird of paradise and another as a gargoyle with a goat head.* NIJINSKY *is very interested in the steps of the tango.)*

(The tango ends and a bolero begins. Couples pair off. The DIAGHELIFF *head approaches* NIJINSKY. *The head is removed and we see the* BARON *underneath.)*

BARON: Good evening. Good evening. How handsome you look, but you're not in costume. Or are you? Let me guess, you're disguised as a gentleman. Just joking. Just joking. As you can see, I've come as a monster our dear Sergei. Speaking of which, I hope you are accepting my proposal. You could work independently. We could build a new theater. Didn't you say you wanted a round theater like the Greeks?

NIJINSKY: Like an eye.

BARON: Yes. Yes. An eye. An eye. Exactly, the cyclopean eye, all seeing. Brilliant. Well, no business. When I hear music...ah...I simply must dance. Do I look like an idiot? Don't tell me if I do. I'm having too much fun!

(The BARON *disappears into the crowd and grabs a partner.* ROMOLA *enters alone. She is wearing an elegant evening dress and her hair is carefully done. She and* NIJINSKY *nod to each other, but stand silently a little ways apart watching the crowd. Finally,* NIJINSKY *moves closer.)*

NIJINSKY: Good evening, *mademoiselle.*

ROMOLA: Good evening, *Monsieur* Nijinsky.

(There is much gesturing and pantomime between them to make themselves understood.)

NIJINSKY: Beautiful dress.

ROMOLA: Thank you.

NIJINSKY: No costume…

ROMOLA: I want to feel pretty, not disguised.

NIJINSKY: For me—Too much costume—always clown, slave, flower—tragic. Tonight only myself.

ROMOLA: Me too.

*(*ROMOLA AND NIJINSKY *smile at each other. They are silent and watch thedance then. They both speak at once.)*

ROMOLA: Do you enjoy…

NIJINSKY: I must tell you.

ROMOLA: Go on. You must tell me… What?

NIJINSKY: No you.

ROMOLA: All right. Do you enjoy this Argentine music?

NIJINSKY: Very much. I learn tango. Very dramatic. You teach?

ROMOLA: I don't know it. I've never been to Buenos Aires before.

(The half-man, half-woman approaches NIJINSKY.*)*

MAN/WOMAN: Senor Nijinsky, I am so honored. I want to prostrate myself before the altar of your magnificence. I want to tell you how noble, how utterly handsome and graceful you are, yet inexorably masculine. Your greatness humbles us all.

NIJINSKY: (*To* ROMOLA) I'm sorry...

ROMOLA: She said she was delighted to meet you.

NIJINSKY: (*He extends his hand, which the* MAN/WOMAN *grabs and kisses.*) You dance very good.

MAN/WOMAN: I hear you love all dances. The tango is queen among dances and, if you like, I will teach you. Yes?

(*They look at* ROMOLA.)

ROMOLA: She'd like to teach you to tango. You see, what you wish for comes true.

NIJINSKY: Now?

ROMOLA: Yes.

(ROMOLA *and* NIJINSKY *stare at each other and reach a silent agreement.*)

NIJINSKY: I love to learn, but later. Tell her please.

ROMOLA: Of course, he'd love to dance, but later.

MAN/WOMAN: Later then. (*She turns the masculine side to him and then the feminine side.*) You can dance with whomever pleases you most. (*She exits.*)

ROMOLA: She said later is fine.

NIJINSKY: You speak Spanish?

ROMOLA: A little.

NIJINSKY: My French—terrible, like savage. You speak Russian?

ROMOLA: Not a word. I don't suppose you speak Hungarian?

NIJINSKY: I am sorry.

ROMOLA: I'm Hungarian. From Budapest.

NIJINSKY: Am Polish and Russian.

ROMOLA: My father's family is from Poland.

NIJINSKY: You speak Polish? I speak Polish.

ROMOLA: No. My father's family left Poland a hundred years ago.

NIJINSKY: Ah.

ROMOLA: Yes.

(They fall silent again. NIJINSKY *offers* ROMOLA *his arm.)*

NIJINSKY: Shall we? Away from lights, see sky better.

*(*ROMOLA *is enchanted. She takes* NIJINSKY*'s arm. They walk a few steps, but it is the dancers who sweep offstage, leaving them alone. The stars brighten and the music grows faint.)*

ROMOLA: Have we crossed… *(Gestures)* Crossed the equator?

NIJINSKY: Yes.

ROMOLA: Then, this is a new sky I've never seen before.

NIJINSKY: The New World.

ROMOLA: They say there are new constellations. New stars that can't be seen from the Northern Hemisphere.

NIJINSKY: You know stars?

ROMOLA: No. Do you know constellations?

NIJINSKY: No.

*(*ROMOLA *and* NIJINSKY *are quiet, smiling for a moment. She turns away and crosses herself.)*

ROMOLA: Thank you Divine Mother.

NIJINSKY: What this?

ROMOLA: Nothing.

NIJINSKY: Tell me, you love dance?

ROMOLA: Dance? Oh dance. I'm only in the chorus.

NIJINSKY: But Ballet Russes chorus! Good. You love dance?

ROMOLA: I adore dance, but…

NIJINSKY: If comes from heart—is good. Others more virtuosi. Yes. But heart give grace.

ROMOLA: If it were only heart you needed! But you work hard at it. Endlessly. I hoped…I thought that grace might be acquired.

NIJINSKY: Ac-quired?

ROMOLA: Learned.

NIJINSKY: Ah yes. Hard work. Good. But grace learned is only little. Grace born. Grace born has no end…

ROMOLA: I should so want grace, limitless grace.

NIJINSKY: So serious. But now we laugh. I show you Dimitri. So vain in his looks—because has none. Now Dimitri in love… Here come man with pipe… (*He mimics* BARON.) I do perfect Dimitri. No?

ROMOLA: Yes. A splendid Dimitri!

(NIJINSKY *walks away suddenly.*)

NIJINSKY: I'm sick of lies.

ROMOLA: What lies?

NIJINSKY: You here with me because I am famous.

ROMOLA: No!

NIJINSKY: Yes. World imitates. Foolish women put eyes like this (*Indicates slanted eyes.*) With black pencil so look like me…ahhh Nijinsky. Ballets Russes— Ooooh-la-la. I am rich now. Famous. If not—you never here!

ROMOLA: How rude!

(ROMOLA *turns to leave.* NIJINSKY *steps in front of her.)*

NIJINSKY: Tell me truth.

ROMOLA: The truth?

NIJINSKY: Yes.

ROMOLA: Fine then. The truth. When I first saw you—you were already rich and famous—so I can't say what I'd have done if you'd been different!

NIJINSKY: Ah!

ROMOLA: Did you understand?

NIJINSKY: Yes. Say again.

ROMOLA: Why?

NIJINSKY: Please.

ROMOLA: I said that when I first say you—you were already rich and famous—so I have no idea what I'd have done if you'd been different.

NIJINSKY: Again!

ROMOLA: Again?

NIJINSKY: Yes. Exact words.

ROMOLA: Why?

NIJINSKY: Like music to me. I love truth. I love this truth.

ROMOLA: What about you? You probably think I am very rich?

NIJINSKY: Yes.

ROMOLA: I'm not very rich. Only a little.

(NIJINSKY *laughs.)*

NIJINSKY: Yes. Yes. (*He is smiling.)*

ROMOLA: What?

NIJINSKY: Now we like Tolstoy and wife Sofia.

ROMOLA: So you've forgiven me Tolstoy?

NIJINSKY: Tolstoy love truth. With truth—open heart. Simple life. Tolstoy and Sofia—write everything… write, write…every morning.

ROMOLA: They kept diaries.

NIJINSKY: Yes. Every night read out loud—everything, good, bad. All. I love this. Peace. And you?

ROMOLA: I don't think I can be so mercilessly candid.

NIJINSKY: Yes. Is possible. Maybe…I begin. No secrets. I am Catholic because born Polish. But really am Russian. Russian soul—eat bread, cabbage soup. I love Russia. I miss Russia too much.

ROMOLA: I'm Catholic too.

NIJINSKY: Yes! Yes! …But…

ROMOLA: But what? Tell me everything.

NIJINSKY: My mother…her mother…

ROMOLA: (*Trying to follow his train of thought)* Your grandmother.

NIJINSKY: Yes. My grandmother die, starve herself. Die screaming.

ROMOLA: How terrible.

NIJINSKY: You must know!

ROMOLA: What?

NIJINSKY: Stassik, my brother…is crazy…ugly. Perhaps I too am… (*He stops, corrects himself. Smiles. He imitates Stassik)*…am good mimic, but great dancer. In dance, I make Stassik beautiful. We talk dance. You are dancer. I must see you dance. If dance, must dance beautifully. I give lessons so you dance more beautifully.

ROMOLA: No. No. I would never even think to ask you.

NIJINSKY: I am not critic. I am teacher. I hate critics. Critics think public is stupid. Critics think to explain art to stupid public. I hate critic. Critic is death. (*He loses himself in thought.)*

ROMOLA: *Monsieur* Nijinsky?

NIJINSKY: Yes.

ROMOLA: Are you all right?

NIJINSKY: I want to say to you, before.

ROMOLA: Yes? What were you going to say?

NIJINSKY: You have beautiful eyes, but is nose I like.

ROMOLA: My nose?

NIJINSKY: (*He kisses her nose.)* Has character. Now know why. Is good straight Polish nose.

(A couple from the dance strolls by. Then the rest of the dancers, a bit inebriated, sweep in. The BARON, *disengages himself and approaches* ROMOLA *and* NIJINSKY.*)*

BARON: Where have you been? You don't know what a stir you've caused. Everyone is talking. So interested. So worried. You, Romuschka are a gold digger and you, Vaslav are a fickle flirt...or is it the other way around?

ROMOLA: I'm afraid that I have a headache that's quite painful. I must find Anna.

BARON: What? I have said something terrible. Don't go. Ignore me. Ah, but, Vatza, can you imagine Sergei? He would be livid. He would be drunk with so many of his English scotches by now, but so polite. He'd kill you with politeness. Thank God, none of us have to worry. He's not here. He's terrified of boats and the ocean. My, ever since a gypsy told him he would die at sea...

NIJINSKY: Excuse, *Mademoiselle*, Baron.

(He goes to the MAN/WOMAN *and asks her to dance. She begins to teach him the tango. The prostitutes also set themselves to learn.)*

BARON: My dear, you must tell me about your evening. Are you in love?

ROMOLA: I must go to bed, Dimitri.

BARON: You're magic together!

ROMOLA: Forgive me.

BARON: But I haven't told you about the other gossip. Poor Maicherska. Did you see? She insisted on displaying her lovely shoulders, even with a tremendous love bite on one of them. She tried to say that a washstand had fallen on her, but no one believed her.

ROMOLA: You must tell me everything. Tomorrow!

BARON: *(As he exits with* ROMOLA*)* I won't hear of it. I shall walk you to your cabin. But, did you hear? One of the busboys cut off the last digit of his ring finger to impress his girlfriend? Such cries…

(The BARON *exits with* ROMOLA.*)*

(End of Scene Five)

Scene Six

*(*ROMOLA *is in her cabin, happy and excited with the evening. She changes into her dressing gown and goes to hang up her dress. She opens a closet, or parts some clothes and there is* EMILIA, *dressed as Ophelia.)*

EMILIA: Well? Who am I?

ROMOLA: Mother!

EMILIA: No, no, no. You know the game. Who am I?

ROMOLA: I'm no longer a child.

EMILIA: That's debatable. But let's not quibble. This is such a good game. Indulge me or I won't go away. Who am I?

ROMOLA: You're Ophelia from The Royal Theater's 1912 production of Hamlet. A very old Ophelia.

EMILIA: If you look as good at my age, you will kneel down and kiss the earth with gratitude. Now what did I do?

ROMOLA: You murdered my father.

EMILIA: Your father killed himself. But I am talking about the play. In the play, what did Ophelia do?

ROMOLA: She died for love. It wasn't reciprocated.

EMILIA: Just like you. I rest my case.

ROMOLA: Like my father.

EMILIA: What would you know? You were a child. Your father was unstable and unpredictable. On a good day, I would say he was a tragic figure, sort of a Don Quixote with a dim sense of reality. On a bad day, I would call him a fool. And when he was drunk…I hated it when Karoly was drunk and wanted to make love…now why are we getting into this?

ROMOLA: We always do.

EMILIA: That's not why I'm here.

ROMOLA: Why are you here?

EMILIA: I won't have you chasing after a man you can never catch. You may despise me, but I am your mother and I warn you, as your mother and as a woman of the world, that Nijinsky's friendship with Diagheliff is more than a friendship. He can't possibly be interested in you!

ROMOLA: Mother—Diagheliff is his past. Perhaps *Le Petit* needs something different now… Why shouldn't I be the one to provide Nijinsky with a future? After all, Diagheliff cannot bear his children!

EMILIA: Oh superb, now you aspire to be a cow's udder.

ROMOLA: Of course that would be how you see mothering…mother! Public acclaim is not my only measure of success.

EMILIA: I don't see you chasing after a bricklayer.

ROMOLA: I aspire to be a person of flesh and blood and heart. I will be passionate and loyal. I will never refuse to go to my husband when he needs me most.

EMILIA: As I did?

ROMOLA: Oh, I understand, Mama. Father was in Australia and, of course, you couldn't go there, could you? After all, you can only act in Hungarian, and Mother—no one understand Hungarian!

EMILIA: All right, then hate me—but don't be a fool.

ROMOLA: Like my father!

EMILIA: Romola!

ROMOLA: Divine Jesus of Prague…please…please… please save me from this horrid woman.

EMILIA: (*Imitates* ROMOLA *scathingly)* Please… Please… Divine Child…

ROMOLA: Go away!

*(*ROMOLA *exits.* ANNA *enters.)*

ANNA: Go away? Go away? And here I thought you wanted to know if your precious Vaslav was on deck. Well he is, and for your information, you only have ten more days to steal his heart. And you needn't be rude to me because you're in a bad mood!

(End of Scene Six)

Scene Seven

(Morning on deck. People coming and going from breakfast. The captain and one of the dancers enter. She is dressed very bohemian for that time. Lots of jewelry and a funky hat)

BOHEMIAN WOMAN: My concepts of society are more developed now. I look at Karl Marx as a very intelligent charismatic revolutionary.

CAPTAIN: Wasn't Karl Marx a Jew?

BOHEMIAN WOMAN: I'm not recanting.

(The BARON *arrives.)*

CAPTAIN: Good morning, Baron.

BARON: Morning, morning.

CAPTAIN: When you sit down, ask for the fresh oranges. Wonderful. Those monkeys in Sicily picked them.

BARON: Gibraltar has the monkeys. Sicily has the oranges.

CAPTAIN: My mistake. I thought those little dark creatures picking oranges in Sicily were monkeys. (*He laughs alone.)*

(CAPTAIN *and the dancer exit.)*

*(*ANNA *arrives and then* RUPERT *close behind her. He offers her a single flower. The* BARON *sees this and stands there glaring at him.)*

ANNA: Rupert. How dear of you. I hope you slept well.

RUPERT: Why is that man staring at me?

ANNA: Perhaps he thinks he knows you.

*(*ANNA *gives a little wave to the* BARON*, who looks away.)*

ANNA: That's Baron de Gunsbourg. He's quite charming, I assure you.

RUPERT: He seems odd, but no matter. How would you like to stroll with me and watch the sun dancing fire off the waves?

ANNA: I'd love to, but I haven't had breakfast yet.

RUPERT: Yes, I see.

ANNA: I'm not rejecting you.

RUPERT: Good. Then, perhaps later this morning.

ANNA: That would be lovely.

RUPERT: Your English is astonishingly good.

ANNA: Why thank you.

RUPERT: Yes, well… Shall I accompany you to breakfast?

ANNA: Why yes.

RUPERT: May I watch you eat?

ANNA: What?

RUPERT: I just thought… The truth is, I find your mouth delectable and want to watch you…well, move it.

ANNA: You're making me quite self-conscious.

RUPERT: Sorry.

ANNA: Yes.

RUPERT: Should I go then?

ANNA: You can stay, but don't stare at my mouth.

RUPERT: Oh, no. I wouldn't think of it.

*(*ANNA *is a bit distracted.)*

RUPERT: There is a favor I'd like to ask.

ANNA: Yes.

RUPERT: The question's been bothering me. Kept me up nights. What a puzzle. And you, being a woman, well, I'm sure you would know this sort of thing.

ANNA: I'd love to help.

RUPERT: Such fine elocution from such a lovely mouth. Sorry. I got carried away. Sorry.

ANNA: Yes.

RUPERT: The question I have is this—well, it's something my aunty told me. She said women stuff all kinds of sweet things inside themselves so animals will lick them down there. Is that true?

ANNA: What!?

*(*ANNA *slaps* RUPERT*'s face and starts to leave.)*

RUPERT: I'll take that as a no.

*(*ANNA *hurries off to* ROMOLA*'s cabin. To* ROMOLA *angrily—)*

ANNA: Loving someone you don't know is a knife in the heart. But I suppose—if a man is twisted or damaged—it is better to know that now.

*(*ROMOLA *comforts her.)*

(End of Scene Seven)

Scene Eight

*(*ROMOLA *and* ANNA *are in* ROMOLA*'s cabin getting ready to go to breakfast.* VASSILY *approaches with a large bouquet of white roses. Two maids rush by, one is carrying clean towels.)*

VASSILY: *(Muttering)* It will be me! Me! I will be the one who answers the door and lies to her annoying face that you're not in! What do you care if you tire of her or not? Everyone wants to see you, meet you, touch you. *(Spits)* What am I, a doorman, a pimp? Wait! You'll see her dance, your heart will drop to your boots and I, Vassily, am here to pick it up and slam the door in her face. Achhh...

*(*VASSILY *knocks loudly on* ROMOLA*'s door.* ANNA *answers.)*

ANNA: Yes?

VASSILY: *(He thrusts the flowers into her arms.)* Here!

*(*VASSILY *walks away a few paces.* ANNA *closes the door, a bit puzzled. She looks for a note.)*

ROMOLA: Who is it?

ANNA: Vassily.

ROMOLA: Oh, let me see. What beautiful roses Anna. You see? I've caught Nijinsky's eye. Isn't it wonderful? Next I'll catch his heart.

*(*VASSILY *knocks again at the door.* ROMOLA *jumps up.* ANNA *opens it. He hands her an envelope. As* ANNA *goes to shut the door, he holds it open.)*

VASSILY: She is very sly, but I know what she is up to. I see everything. How she talks louder when he enters a room so he'll notice her. How she waits to come out her door until he's in the hallway. She can never understand him. Never. He was born to dance. She is nothing. She will never know his true heart. My God, she will ruin him. Sergei Diagheliff will have a heart attack. It is the end of the Ballets Russes. *Finis!* *(He is almost in tears. He exits.)*

ANNA: *(Yells after him.)* *Moujik!* *(She slams the door.)*

ROMOLA: What did he say?

ANNA: Don't ask me. I don't understand a word of that barbaric language. All I understood was *"finis"* and he gave me this. It's for you, of course.

ROMOLA: *"Finis? Finis?"* What does he mean finished?

ANNA: Go ahead. Read it to me.

ROMOLA: Just a minute. (*She smells it.*) Mmm. It has his cologne, Guerlain, I believe.

ANNA: I prefer the smell of pipe tobacco and a good energetic walk around the deck. (*Referring to the note*) If the French is good, you can be sure the Baron wrote it.

ROMOLA: Oh.

ANNA: What does it say?

ROMOLA: He says "forgive me". But I have nothing to forgive him for. What could he mean? He's sorry he kissed me. He won't be seeing me again. "*Finis*." "*Finis.*" What else could it mean?

ANNA: Ask him.

ROMOLA: I can't face him.

ANNA: I can't stand it. Let's go to breakfast. Please. I'm starving and Nijinsky has already left. I heard his door close.

ROMOLA: I'll die if he ignores me when I pass his table. I'll know he meant good-bye. And after they all saw us alone together. The humiliation. Everyone will see it. No, I can't possibly go.

ANNA: Young love is so enervating. You really must come out and eat something.

ROMOLA: You go. At least I can practice. I must practice. I must dance.

*(*ANNA *exits as* ROMOLA *begins to practice. She starts with some hesitant steps from* Les Sylphides*. The two women dancers come out in classic white tutus and proceed to dance* Sylphides *beautifully.* ROMOLA *tries to keep up with them. She can't. She watches sadly and then exits. This dance should be almost a minute and a half.)*

END OF ACT ONE

ACT TWO

Scene One

(It is late night. ROMOLA *is pacing the deck. A couple passes sees her and starts whispering. She turns away and cries silently. The* CAPTAIN *with a bottle of champagne rushes through, stops for a minute, unsure if he should go to* ROMOLA *or not. Decides better of it and exits.* ROMOLA *sits on a deck chair in the dark and lights a cigarette.* NIJINSKY *enters.)*

NIJINSKY: *Mademoiselle!*

ROMOLA: (*Startled, she is torn between wanting to run away and putting out her cigarette. She does neither.)* Go away.

NIJINSKY: Romola.

ROMOLA: What?!

NIJINSKY: Smoke, no good for dance. (*Mimes coughing)*

ROMOLA: Leave if it bothers you. *(She turns so he can't see her face. She blows a plume of smoke.)*

NIJINSKY: Eyes red.

ROMOLA: Please, *Monsieur* Nijinsky.

NIJINSKY: You like me little, so can't say, Vaslav?

ROMOLA: We hardly know each other.

NIJINSKY: True. We walk and know better.

ROMOLA: No, thank you. (*She puts out her cigarette.)*

NIJINSKY: You cry?

ROMOLA: No.

NIJINSKY: I see. But, I think you cry. I think. I think… *(He kisses her lightly.)* You cry for me?

ROMOLA: Yes. So?

NIJINSKY: We walk.

ROMOLA: Please spare me. Well, leave! Or do you think I'm so desperate that common decency won't work with me? You're probably right, I'm like one of those silly girls who steal your underwear after a performance. And yes, I've done that too. I've rummaged around in your hotel at Monte Carlo—like an opium addict after cash… I snatched a little pillow they said your mother made which you slept on every night. So there! I stole it! I sleep with it. So—laugh at me!

NIJINSKY: *(Laughing)* I'm sorry. You speak too fast. You love a pillow?

ROMOLA: You're impossible. You understood every word I said.

NIJINSKY: No. Please, please. Not words. But, you I understand. I feel you. You feel me, too, no? So.

(NIJINSKY takes ROMOLA's hand and puts it through his arm. They walk. he points to the sky.)

NIJINSKY: That? So bright. The Southern Cross. See, I have learned. New World.

(NIJINSKY and ROMOLA watch the sky in silence for a moment. We hear the water against the hull of the moving ship.)

NIJINSKY: Modern people say no God. Everything "little pieces in motion". I believe in God. Some people God wants… *(Gestures)*…together. In the Stars. (He holds their hands out together. He points to her ring finger, and then to his.) Romola?

ROMOLA: Yes.

NIJINSKY: Do you want? *Voulez-vous? Vous et moi?*

ROMOLA: You and I?

NIJINSKY: Yes.

ROMOLA: Married?

NIJINSKY: *Oui.*

(Extended pause between them. A group of four approach. Three women draping themselves over the arm of a tall man in a top hat. The women are laughing.)

NIJINSKY: You first woman I love.

ROMOLA: The very first?

NIJINSKY: Yes.

ROMOLA: I don't believe you.

NIJINSKY: Truth.

ROMOLA: But you're in such carefree company with so many beautiful women!

NIJINSKY: But only you. Only. (*He kisses her hand.) Voulez-vous? Vous et moi? …Oui?*

ROMOLA: Yes. Oh yes. I'll marry you!

*(*NIJINSKY *kisses* ROMOLA*'s hand again, then kisses her.)*

ROMOLA: But when?

NIJINSKY: Now. Buenos Aires. Sacred. In church.

ROMOLA: Yes. In church. A dress! I have no papers! (*She embraces him.)* I knew you had a kind heart. I saw you dance so many, many times. I knew your genius, your nature, everything! Anyone who dances as you do must have a loving heart!

NIJINSKY: I am sorry…

ROMOLA: But, *Monsieur*...what do you want from me?

NIJINSKY: From you...?

ROMOLA: *Monsieur.*

NIJINSKY: Yes?

ROMOLA: Why did you write "forgive me" on the note with your flowers?

NIJINSKY: (*Laughs)* Dark mood. Russian mood. But at heart—am joyous Pole. So! Now—only beautiful notes. I go write—dancing like Pavlova. (*He imitates Pavolva and glides offstage.)*

(End of Scene One)

Scene Two

*(*ROMOLA *is trying on dresses.* ANNA *is helping her.* ANNA *exits.* EMILIA *enters, dressed exotically and tragically as Medea.)*

EMILIA: Ouff—don't tell me you're wearing blue. It's very unlucky.

ROMOLA: For the love of God!

EMILIA: You know who I am today, or do I need to show you my bloody knife?

ROMOLA: Why would you come to my marriage as Medea, mother?

EMILIA: Marriage can be vicious.

ROMOLA: You're jealous because I've proven you wrong. He can love me. He does love me.

EMILIA: I wouldn't wear blue if I were you.

*(*EMILIA *drifts offstage crossing paths with two ballerinas who rush in.)*

BALLERINA 1: Katrina is having hysterics because Nijinsky is marrying you. And, with all the men on board, she has to faint in my husband's arms.

BALLERINA 2: Congratulations! I am so happy. So happy for you. I always knew Nijinsky wasn't like that. Let me see your ring.

(She does.)

BALLERINA 2: Very pretty.

BALLERINA 1: For my part, I would rather be a mistress. The Aga Kahn sent Marushka seven leopard skins and a ruby belt because she had the sniffles. Of course, Marushka is a *prima ballerina.*

BALLERINA 2: Ouff! Don't tell me you're wearing blue. That's very unlucky.

(They exit whispering together and ANNA *returns with some pins to pin up the dress.)*

ROMOLA: I can't stand that dress.

ANNA: Why not? We're almost finished.

ROMOLA: I hate it. I won't wear it. Blue is bad luck.

ANNA: So, now you're superstitious?

ROMOLA: Now is not the time to tempt the gods. I want the white dress. With ropes of pearls.

ANNA: Well, you can't wear pearls.

ROMOLA: Why not?

ANNA: Some say they're unlucky too.

ROMOLA: Then I won't get married at all. Forget it!

ANNA: You don't mean that.

ROMOLA: Why not? I'm frightened. What's going to happen? Who knows what marriage is! I know—I'll write a note. Yes—find me some note paper. I'll write him. Ah, yes, I'll begin… "Forgive me…"

ANNA: Don't be ridiculous. It's only nerves.

ROMOLA: But it's not! What's the use? It's a farce.

ANNA: Roma—he loves you.

ROMOLA: But he hasn't seen me dance.

*(*ANNA *exits and returns with a cream-colored dress. At first,* ROMOLA *refuses to put it on, but then grudgingly lets* ANNA *dress her.)*

*(*NIJINSKY *in his wedding tuxedo takes him place on one corner of the stage. The priest appears in the center.* EMILIA *enters still dressed as Medea.)*

EMILIA: September 10, 1913. The first marriage—*le mariage du coeur*. Ladies and gentlemen, (*Indicating the wedding)* the Tower of Babel. The priest is speaking Latin; Romola, Hungarian; *Le Petit* Nijinsky, Polish. I have a headache and I'm not even invited.

(As EMILIA *exits, a vast shower of flower petals fall. The dancers enter carrying small lights which they place on the floor.* ROMOLA *has put on an extraordinarily long veil which trails behind her. She takes her place in another corner of the stage. As she and* NIJINSKY *speak, they walk towards each other. They are extremely happy.)*

ROMOLA: I, Romola, will stay with you, Vaslav, in happiness and misfortune, in health and sickness till death do us part

NIJINSKY: I, Vaslav, will stay with you, Romola, in happiness and misfortune, in health and sickness till death do us part.

(They exchange rings.)

P<P8>RIEST<P10>: In the name of The Father, The Son, and The Holy Spirit, I now pronounce you man and wife. Let no man put asunder whom God has joined today.

(They kiss. NIJINSKY *carries* ROMOLA *to the hotel room. There is a splendidly made up bed and an ornate chair with a robe lying over it and some books on the floor. The dancers scamper ahead and explore* NIJINSKY'*s hotel room,bounce on the bed and look in every corner. One picks up a book that is lying around. The other one slaps her and takes it away and puts it back. They exit annoyed with each other .)*

(End of Scene Two)

Scene Three

(Hotel suite in Buenos Aires. ROMOLA *and* NIJINSKY *enter.)*

NIJINSKY: *(With grand gesture)* Honeyroom.

ROMOLA: *(Laughing)* Honey-moon.

(They laugh together. ROMOLA *looks over everything, touches a wall, a chair, etc.* NIJINSKY *watches. She comes to a robe draped over the bed and some books nearby.)*

NIJINSKY: I have champagne.

*(*NIJINSKY *exits to get it.* ROMOLA *touches his things—the valise, smells his robe, picks up one of the books to look at it. He enters with an open bottle and glasses. She takes them from him and fills the glasses.)*

ROMOLA: Let me pour.

NIJINSKY: *(He kisses her neck.) Maia jena.*

ROMOLA: What does that mean?

NIJINSKY: My wife.

*(*ROMOLA *and* NIJINSKY *smile at each other. He dips a finger in the Champagne and traces a cross on her forehead.)*

NIJINSKY: My mother always bless. "Christ be with you."

ROMOLA: And also with you.

NIJINSKY: Ah yes...and "Together forever through fire and water"!

ROMOLA: Is that holy too.

NIJINSKY: No. Polish.

ROMOLA: *(She dips her finger in the Champagne and makes the sing of the cross over his heart.)* "May this blessing preserve you from all evil". There! You're safe! My family says that—in Hungarian mind you!

*(*ROMOLA *and* NIJINSKY *sip their champagne.)*

ROMOLA: Now what shall we do?

NIJINSKY: We marry fast. Now—slow. slow. Roma, Romuscka, I have plan.

ROMOLA: Tell me.

NIJINSKY: Four years I dance, I live only for art. Then five years go to Russia, make a school, make children, make real family. I think is very good. And you?

ROMOLA: It's a wonderful plan. I'm so happy. We'll travel and entertain. We'll read Russian novels and tour museums and, of course, I will dress extravagantly well. And so will you— *(She brings over the robe.)* Put on the present I bought you. I want to see how you look!

NIJINSKY: Yes.

(As NIJINSKY *tries on the robe* ROMOLA *looks through the books.)*

ROMOLA: Does it fit? Put it on. No. You have to take your jacket off first. There. *(She puts down the book and helps him.)* Now your bowtie... *(She helps him.)*...and your cummerbund...no, I'll let you do that.

*(*NIJINSKY *takes off his cummerbund and puts on the robe.)*

ROMOLA: You look like an emperor...I know...the emperor of Mongolia!

(ROMOLA pulls the skin near her eyes to make them slant. They both laugh. She holds up the book.)

ROMOLA: Is this yours?

NIJINSKY: Yes.

(NIJINSKY goes to take it from ROMOLA.)

ROMOLA: I want to see what you're reading.

NIJINSKY: Better no.

ROMOLA: I want to know all about you! I'm your wife now. And it's only a book. Oh! A picture book. It's Chinese. How exotic.

(One of the dancers steals in and reads over her shoulder. The other dancer comes in shyly, curious.)

NIJINSKY: It is very old.

ROMOLA: Look how beautiful it's made. All the figures are hand painted. The writing's so black, but it's Chinese. I can't read it.

(The two dancers assume an obviously sexual pose and then contort into another. They laugh and run off as ROMOLA says.)

ROMOLA: They're having sex!

NIJINSKY: I wanted for… You are offended.

ROMOLA: No. It's funny. It's fascinating…once you get used to it.

NIJINSKY: Like you.

(NIJINSKY kisses ROMOLA. They kiss and become passionate. He helps her out of her dress. He has her stand in her underclothes. They kiss again. He turns her gently around and kneels and caresses her buttocks softly and rests his head against her. DIAGHELIFF enters.)

DIAGHELIFF: Have you forgotten, you're the god of dance? Get off your knees and get some rest, and for God's sake, make her shave her pubis!

*(*DIAGHELIFF *exits.* NIJINSKY *rises.)*

ROMOLA: What? But where are you going? Vaslav. Vaslav?

*(*NIJINSKY *is frightened. He starts to leave.)*

ROMOLA: Don't go. We must sleep together. Only people who fall asleep and wake up together really belong to each other.

NIJINSKY: *(Kisses her hand)* Forgive me. *(He exits.)*

(End of Scene Three)

Scene Four

*(*ROMOLA *is doing warm-up exercises in her room. She is in practice clothes. In another part of the stage is the rehearsal area. We see a barre and hear a piano offstage where an accompanist is playing Stravinsky.* NIJINSKY *paces.)*

*(*VASSILY *knocks on* ROMOLA*'s door and when she answers motions for her to follow him.)*

VASSILY: Come!

ROMOLA: Where?

VASSILY: *Monsieur* Nijinsky. Practice.

ROMOLA: Rehearsal isn't for two hours!

VASSILY: Rehearsal, no. Class.

ROMOLA: He wants to see me dance?

*(*VASSILY *shrugs.)*

ROMOLA: Now?

VASSILY: Yes.

ROMOLA: (*Looks around wildly)* I can't.

VASSILY: Good. (*He smirks and leaves.)*

ROMOLA: Oh God!

*(*ROMOLA *runs after* VASSILY *crossing herself repeatedly. In the rehearsal room* VASSILY *enters and waits for* NIJINSKY *to finish.)*

NIJINSKY: No. What are you thinking? Stop! (*He paces.)* It's *presto prestissimo.* One and two and three and four five, one and two and three and four five. You're playing like you're dragging a dead horse. I can't believe you've played for the greatest dancers of the Ballets Russes. One and two and three and four five. Play it as Stravinsky wrote it. He is a musical genius, you are not!

*(*ROMOLA *enters, ready to greet* NIJINSKY. *He ignores her.)*

NIJINSKY: Enough! We have an opening tomorrow. Do you want to ruin everything? Go practice where I can't hear you. *Prestissimo, prestissimo,* cretin! Go ahead. Go!

*(*VASSILY *is about to speak with* NIJINSKY *when the* BARON *pops in.)*

BARON: (*Popping in for a minute)* The girls are hysterical. We opened the trunks and the dresser packed only half the shoes. Arkady has a splinter in his foot and can't dance and all the doctors are at Mass. Oh, yes, they're sanding the stage floor so we can't possibly get in until four…which really means seven if we're lucky. It's a disaster. Why am I doing this? …Sorry to bother you. *(He exits.)*

ROMOLA: (*Steps close to* NIJINSKY *and whispers)* You sent for me.

NIJINSKY: Vassily, come here. Please ask Toussia to come down in an hour. We'll practice our *pas de deux.*

VASSILY: I would like to watch this practice.

NIJINSKY: I don't care particularly what you would like this morning, Vassily.

VASSILY: Very good, sir. An hour then? Won't you need two or three—with her?!

NIJINSKY: Vassily! Go!

*(*VASSILY *bows and exits.)*

ROMOLA: He loathes me. He was the only person in the entire company who didn't come to our wedding.

NIJINSKY: Forget about it. It's nothing. We have an opening tomorrow. An opening is fate. It's everything. We win the audience. Or not. There are no second chances. What was I thinking? I should have seen you dance sooner!

ROMOLA: You're speaking in Russian, Vaslav.

NIJINSKY: The dance needs precision, refinement. The slightest deviation, the smallest undue tension in the rhythm of the movement, any small mistake can destroy the whole composition. The dance becomes a caricature.

ROMOLA: Vaslav, I can't understand you.

NIJINSKY: I give class. Go to barre.

*(*ROMOLA *goes to the barre and does some stretches and pliés, loosening up.* EMILIA *and* DIAGHELIFF *enter.* DIAGHELIFF *is being very gallant. He bows and lets her enter first. He is in evening dress, and* EMILIA *is costumed as Medea.* NIJINSKY *moves over to watch* ROMOLA.*)*

NIJINSKY: *(Gently)* Close to fifth. Now! *Grande developpe en croix.* Leg up. Hold. Turn out. Turn out.

ROMOLA: My leg is already turned out.

NIJINSKY: No. Wrong. Must begin here. *(He adjusts her.)* Yes. Pelvis move forward and heel correct. Yes. There. Very good.

DIAGHELIFF: What did you expect? An artist to share your heart and soul? My poor Vaslav. Tsk, tsk, tsk.

EMILIA: She's quite good and quite beautiful.

DIAGHELIFF: *Madame*, she has no rhythm. A dancer without rhythm is a freak.

NIJINSKY: Arabesesque. Stretch. *Stretch.* Reach for rubies, diamonds, reach! Good. (*To* DIAGHELIFF.) You're jealous of my beautiful bride. Admit it, Sergei. (*To* ROMOLA) Now *cloche. Soutenus.* Feet together. Hold. Stay. (*To* DIAGHELIFF) You will be happy for me even though you can't love this way. She is brutal and sweet. Her eyes are blue green like the sea at Lido. Think of the Lido, Sergei, where you find all your beautiful little Italian boys stretched out on the beach, powdered with sand as if they are delectable blini covered with sugar. You will forgive me.

DIAGHELIFF: Never! You'll make babies, not ballets!

NIJINSKY: (*To* ROMOLA) *Plié* and *pique arabsesque.* Hold. *Paulement! Paulement!* Head like this—cheek rest on soft pillow. Again!

(ROMOLA *continues.*)

NIJINSKY: Too hard *Madame.* Not gorilla. Girl! Must be—light, light-stepping on eggs with no breaking. Again. No. No. Walk please.

ROMOLA: Walk?

NIJINSKY: Yes. Walk now.

ROMOLA: Have I done something wrong?

NIJINSKY: No. Walk, please. Away. Stop. Loose. Now walk. Not in *danse de style.* (*He takes first one hand and then the other and shakes it hard.*) Fingers close. Natural. (*He takes her hand again and shakes it harder.*) For beautiful hands, watch children. Children natural always. Walk. *Madame*, concentrate!

ROMOLA: (*To* EMILIA*)* Am I doing badly?

EMILIA: (*Staring at* DIAGHELIFF*)* Who wouldn't with all this faggotry!

DIAGHELIFF: (*To* EMILIA*)* Does he really know what it means to cross me? And to cross me like this? For a cow? I could almost cry for his ignorance. (*He turns his back.)*

NIJINSKY: Stop. You work too hard.

ROMOLA: You told me to work hard!

NIJINSKY: Dance not work. You are too tight. You move like cripple.

ROMOLA: I'm about to die from nerves. Of course I'm tight, but you can't understand because you're a machine, not a human being!

NIJINSKY: Dance never tight. (*He speaks in Russian out of frustration.)* Dance is simple. Like one breath and then another. Every step, every action is separate, but it must seem inevitable.

ROMOLA: Please speak French, Vaslav.

NIJINSKY: Ach! (*He walks away.)*

ROMOLA: Mother, what have I done?

EMILIA: Romuschka, I'm afraid for you.

ROMOLA: Don't say that. Why do you say that?

EMILIA: Look at him.

ROMOLA: He's an artist that's all and he's Russian!

EMILIA: Romola, his grandmother went mad and starved herself to death—

ROMOLA: So? Papa killed himself and I'm not insane.

EMILIA: He has a brother who sits drooling in a lunatic asylum.

ROMOLA: Stassik fell two stories and damaged his head. Everyone knows that.

EMILIA: You want to be his nursemaid the rest of your life. Is this what you aspire to?

ROMOLA: Why can't you just be happy for me and not state your cruel intentions as if they were prophecies? Everything will be splendid mother. I'd die for him!

EMILIA: One doesn't have to die for love, for love to be real.

ROMOLA: Papa did!

EMILIA: Enough! Enough! Your father didn't die for love. He died for greed. He embezzled money. It was a great scandal.

ROMOLA: You lie. You're lying.

EMILIA: And you can stop blaming me for your father's death. It wasn't I who placed a gun in his hand and made him blow his brains out. It was his so-called friends in Budapest who gave him the revolver and suggested that he end his life honorably.

ROMOLA: Why are you saying this?

EMILIA: To save you. Please. Leave Nijinsky…and if you are pregnant—have an abortion.

*(*EMILIA *exits.* ROMOLA *goes to* NIJINSKY.*)*

ROMOLA: What shall I do?

NIJINSKY: *(Not looking at her)* Dance. Dance. You may weep, but you must work. Even for the very back row of the *Corps de Ballet*. Dance. An artist must have one goal, one goal only—to perfect himself, to attain new heights in his art. Always, always.

*(*NIJINSKY *turns, hoping to be embraced by* DIAGHELIFF, *who stands back.)*

NIJINSKY: What have I done? What have I done? She is not a dancer. I've thrown my life away!

DIAGHELIFF: Good! Suffer! Die! I look at you and glass explodes in my heart. You want to puncture my heart and kill me? I can't endure this. I won't work with you. I can't work with you. I don't need you. There are stables full of young men. Academies! And, if they are not geniuses, they are beautiful and talented. The public will hardly know the difference. (*He exits.*)

(End of Scene Four)

Scene Five

*(*ANNA *is standing outside* NIJINSKY*'s room. The* BARON *joins her.)*

BARON: Am I late? Well, it's no wonder. I've just discovered the world's greatest work of fiction—our contract with the theater! Nothing is true. Nothing! They promised us twenty musicians and we have five who speak God only knows what language. Yes, there are bathrooms, but none of them work and three dancers have diarrhea. I'm beginning to detest producing. It's debasing. Where is Romola and how are you, my dear?

ANNA: (*A little testy.*) I'm fine, Baron. Romola should be here any minute.

(The CAPTAIN *walks by rapidly with a suitcase that is far too heavy for him. The* MAN WITH THE PIPE *comes by arm in arm with an older, obviously wealthy woman who has a cane. They stop to confer together nearby. Both* BARON *and* ANNA *stare at them. The* MAN WITH THE PIPE *and the woman then stroll by. Neither gives* ANNA *nor* BARON *a glance.)*

ANNA: I hate the English.

BARON: Yes. Despicable.

ANNA: Do you know that man?

BARON: What man? Where? Which man?

ANNA: That man with the pipe.

BARON: Oh, no. Never met him.

ANNA: Don't bother. He's a sadist.

(ROMOLA enters.)

ROMOLA: Thank God you're here, Dimitri. I couldn't do this without you! (*Takes out a cigarette and lights it)* This will be my last cigarette.

BARON: Gracious, you sound like a condemned prisoner…

ANNA: I've left your bags. Do you need me for anything else?

ROMOLA: No. Thank you Anna….we might as well go in now.

BARON: Yes…but…

(ROMOLA goes to put out the cigarette but ANNA takes it.)

ANNA: Here, I'll take it.

(Both the BARON and ROMOLA look at her in astonishment as she takes a puff.)

ANNA: Ahh, camel dung! (*She exits.)*

(The BARON and ROMOLA enter the honeymoon suite. VASSILY advises NIJINSKY of their arrival. NIJINSKY enters from the bedroom.)

BARON: Vaslav, so good to see you. What a lovely suite. Oh, and a view from the harbor. My, my, doesn't that street down there remind you of that little section of Paris with all the strange shops. You know the one—where you can buy a new cranial saw or a wax model of a human nose complete with hair.

(NIJINSKY *isn't responding.)*

BARON: You did know I was coming?

NIJINSKY: *(To* ROMOLA*)* Why the Baron?

ROMOLA: Yes, well…there are some private things to say, but obviously, we must understand everything between us…so I've brought the Baron.

BARON: Yes, you see, she said that this is rather embarrassing, but…

NIJINSKY: Please, Dimitri. Don't insult me. I can look at her face and understand.

BARON: He says to continue.

ROMOLA: I'm nervous.

NIJINSKY: Tell her, she must talk without stopping. I am very nervous.

BARON: Vaslav asks that you speak freely.

ROMOLA: I can guess what he said. It's not so easy to speak as he supposes. *(She faces* NIJINSKY *directly.)* First, what did you think of my dancing? Will I ever dance like Pavlova, like Karsavina?

NIJINSKY: No, never.

BARON: Why not? She's very lithe and graceful.

NIJINSKY: *(To* ROMOLA*)* You begin too late.

ROMOLA: I understand.

NIJINSKY: But, I compose special little dances for you dance beautifully.

ROMOLA: Don't bother. I will never dance in public again.

NIJINSKY: That's stupid *(To* BARON*)* Tell her an artist can never…

ROMOLA: An artist what? I'm not an artist. God, I'm so sick of hearing this!

BARON: You have to go slower. He'll never understand you and he all but forbids me to translate! This is a disaster.

NIJINSKY: How can I love you if you are not an artist? An artist can traverse a whole world—by pacing from one wall of a room to the other. You see only four walls. A prison. I can't live like that! I asked you to learn to dance, because for me, dancing is the highest art. I wanted to teach you, but you became frightened. You didn't trust me. At that moment, I felt death. I had put myself in the hands of someone who could never comprehend me.

BARON: Vaslav wants you to dance.

NIJINSKY: Baron, *stop!*

ROMOLA: Then it's settled. You can't love me. We shall get an annulment!

BARON: This is impossible. I cannot be put in this situation! Vaslav, be reasonable. I must translate. These are very delicate matters. How will you understand each other?

*(*NIJINSKY *turns his back.)*

BARON: Romola Carlovna, what am I to do? Please I beg you—both of you—come to some agreement. Surely something can be done.

*(*ROMOLA *is silent.)*

BARON: And now what? What shall I do? What shall I tell Diagheliff? Oh yes, Sergei—or had you forgotten? I just wired him that you are married. He'll be in shock. He's most likely writhing on the floor in paroxysms of rage as we speak. Now he must be told something else? What?

NIJINSKY: Why don't we tell him about our intimate little dance company, Baron?

BARON: No, no, no… That's impossible. He must not know me for the idiot that I am. I tell you I am haunted by stupidity. I scarcely have the character for my own relationships, let alone an entire company of them. I don't know how Sergei does it. (*He looks from one to the other. He shrugs.*) I suppose I shall have to ask him…if he is still speaking to me! (*He exits.*)

ROMOLA: Did you understand what I said? We haven't slept together. The Catholic Church will grant us an annulment.

NIJINSKY: Yes. I know this "annulment". I will do what God tells me. (*He closes his eyes.*)

ROMOLA: Do what your heart tells you.

(NIJINSKY *moves toward* ROMOLA *and cups her cheek with his hand.*)

NIJINSKY: Only God knows our heart.

ROMOLA: How can you think that,Vaslav? People don't love each other because of the love of God or the fear of God. We love someone because the world doesn't make sense if we don't.

NIJINSKY: Sense! What sense! (*He laughs softly.*) Roma, Romuschka, you are a dangerous girl for me. You have the willfulness of a rich girl. You live entitled, oblivious but you suffer. You love me and I am drawn to you with iron straps. Who knows what it is. You are innocent and wicked and brave. And you're beautiful. You are more beautiful than you are supposed to be. So beautiful that you should be stupid, but you're not stupid. I love you.

(NIJINSKY *kisses* ROMOLA. *She kisses him. He holds her fiercely.*)

ROMOLA: What is it, Vaslav?

NIJINSKY: You need words. I don't have them. I am a lullabyer. Rockabye, bye, bye, bye. Rockabye, bye, bye rockabye bye bye, rockabye bye bye. (*He continues hypnotized by his own words.)*

ROMOLA: Vaslav. Please.

(The dancers enter. The following dance should last about two minutes. As they dance—they encircle the couple in tighter and tighter circles and two of the dancers finally dance the couple offstage. The third dancer lays out a huge cross. The other two dancers come out with candles or small magical lights of some kind, genuflect and place them near the foot of the cross and exit. Other lights appear like eyes, some blinking, some staring, some human, some non-human.)

(End of Scene Five)

Scene Six

*(*EMILIA *enters dressed soberly for winter.* ROMOLA *enters also dressed for a concert in winter. She carries an ornate chair and places it near center sage facing the audience. She retreats and waits—looking towards the wings.* NIJINSKY *stalks out angrily and sits in the chair staring challengingly at the audience.)*

EMILIA: The second marriage, *le mariage avec dieu.* Who was invited? January 19th, 1919. A private recital. Saint Moritz Switzerland.

*(*EMILIA *exits.* ROMOLA *is disturbed watching* NIJINSKY. *She darts apprehensive glances at the audience. She goes over to him.)*

ROMOLA: Vaslav, please tell me what the pianist should play for you.

NIJINSKY: Quiet. Do not speak.

*(*ROMOLA *retreats.)*

NIJINSKY: I used to deceive my wife because I had too much semen. I had to ejaculate. I liked whores, but did not ejaculate into them. I have lots of semen and I keep it for another child. I hope I will be presented with the gift of a boy. God is a prick who breeds with one woman. I am a man who breeds children with one woman. I used to give my wife roses that cost five francs a piece. I brought her roses every day—twenty, thirty at a time. I loved giving her white roses. Red roses frightened me. I loved her terribly, but already I felt death. My wife wept and wept. She suffered. I wanted a simple life. I loved Tolstoy. I loved the dance. I wanted to work. I worked hard. I was like a draft horse, whipped until it fell to its knees and all its guts dropped out its ass. I lost heart. I noticed I wasn't liked. I weep and I weep. I love Tolstoy. I love Russia, although I am a Catholic Pole. I will work on a farm. I will practice masturbation and spiritualism. I will eat everyone I can get a hold of. I will stop at nothing. I will make love to my wife's mother and my child. I will weep, but I will do everything God commands me. (*A moment of sanity)* No! I do not love anyone. I am evil. I wish to harm everyone and be good to myself. I am an egoist. I am not God. I am a beast and a predator.

(ROMOLA *approaches cautiously, giving the audience anxious looks as if to invite their sympathy or understanding.)*

ROMOLA: Please, won't you begin *Sylphides*?

NIJINSKY: How dare you disturb me? I am not a machine. I will dance when I feel like it! (*To the audience)* You are stupid. You are beasts. You are meat. You are death. I feel God. I feel God. You came to be amused, but God wants to arouse you. I will dance frightening things. See? I can mimic a crazy person like my brother Stassik. I can be a whore, an old Jew with peyes, a cripple, an aristocrat. (*Looking around for the voices)* Who says workmen are good? Workmen are as depraved as aristocrats. They have less money. They drink cheap wine. My stomach is clean. I do not like meat. I saw how a calf was killed. I saw how a pig was killed. I saw it and felt their tears. I could not bear it.

See?

I can dance like a dying pig, like a dying Czar, like a soldier creeping in the shadow of the gate and shot— "unh" —in the snow. (*In his mind he hears a voice. he is joyful.)* Ay, I feel God. He loves me. I love him. Today… Today… Silence… (*He listens. He hears something, but it's not what he wants.)* Silence! Today is the day of my marriage with God!

*(*NIJINSKY *throws himself to the ground and makes fucking motions to the floor—a distortion of the ending of* L'Apres Midi. ROMOLA *covers her face.)*

END OF PLAY

www.ingramcontent.com/pod-product-compliance
Ingram Content Group UK Ltd.
Pitfield, Milton Keynes, MK11 3LW, UK
UKHW020136250726
13967UKWH00002B/692